PEANUTS

SNOOPY and WOODSTOCK
Best Friends Forever!

by Charles M. Schulz

adapted by Tina Gallo

illustrated by Robert Pope

Ready-to-Read

Simon Spotlight

New York   London   Toronto   Sydney   New Delhi

SIMON SPOTLIGHT
An imprint of Simon & Schuster Children's Publishing Division
1230 Avenue of the Americas, New York, New York 10020
This Simon Spotlight edition October 2020
© 2018 Peanuts Worldwide LLC
For information about special discounts for bulk purchases, please contact Simon & Schuster Special Sales at
1-866-506-1949 or business@simonandschuster.com.
Manufactured in the United States of America 0421 LAK
4 6 8 10 9 7 5 3
ISBN 978-1-5344-0977-4 (eBook)
ISBN 978-1-5344-7333-1 (prop)

Snoopy and Woodstock are best friends.

They play together.

They share secrets.

They share snacks.

But how did they meet?
When did they become friends?

Woodstock chirps at Snoopy.
Snoopy speaks fluent bird.
He understands exactly what
Woodstock is saying.

"You want to hear the story of
how we met? Okay!" Snoopy says.
Snoopy goes into his doghouse
and comes back out with a photo
album.

"One day I woke up from a nap and discovered someone had built a nest on my stomach," Snoopy says.

"I thought to myself,
the next thing you know,
there will be . . .

Baby birds!

"Those baby birds were cute, but they chirped all day and all night long," Snoopy continues.

"So I would gently hum a sweet song, and after a little while, both baby birds would fall asleep.

"I kept waiting for the baby birds to fly away. But there was just one problem. They didn't know how to fly!

"I was getting impatient. They kept trying fancy moves. They would stand on my nose and flap their wings. I wanted them to just fly away!

"Finally, one of the birds
just took off! I was so happy.
'Go, bird, go!' I cheered.

"But he was back almost immediately.

"The next thing I knew he was hanging on to my nose with all his might, as if he never wanted to let go.

"The next time the birds tried to fly,
I took their nest so they could not
come back.

"'Go, birds, go! You're on your own!'
I shouted. I waved good-bye. They
were shocked, to say the least."

Woodstock chirps at Snoopy. He
knew Woodstock was asking
him what happened next.
"I started to feel a little guilty,"
Snoopy says.

"I felt bad for making the birds leave their home so soon.

"But then I looked up and thought that they were probably up in the clouds somewhere, flying and having a good time.

"I was wrong!

"One bird kept coming back, again and again," Snoopy continued. He smiles at Woodstock. "It was you!" Snoopy says.

Woodstock tells Snoopy he doesn't
know what kind of bird he is.
Does Snoopy?
"I'm not sure," Snoopy tells him.

"I know you're not an eagle, because
you don't like heights," Snoopy says.

"And you're not a duck," Snoopy
continues, "because you can't
swim. So I don't know what kind of
bird you are either."

But to these buddies, it really doesn't matter what kind of bird Woodstock is.

Because Snoopy and Woodstock
will always be best friends forever!